THINK DOG

HOW TO BE THE BEST

THE NEVER BEFORE TOLD SECRETS
OF A REAL LIFE 'TOP DOG'

Will and Annalese Murray

Friendly
Publishing
Ltd

First published in 2005 by
Friendly Publishing
PO Box 192
Evesham
Worcestershire WR11 7WW
UK
www.friendlypublishing.com

ISBN 0-9550897-1-9

Text design and typesetting by Sparks – www.sparks.co.uk
Cover design by Murray Murray – www.murraymurray.com

Printed and bound in Great Britain by Acorn Press Ltd, Swindon

To George and Henry

We know you can do it!
Celebrate talent
Lead by example
Be relentless
Make time for those you love

Many thanks
Thank you to Tom at Sparks and
Keith at Acorn Press for their
help in turning this book from an
idea into a reality.

Thank you to our parents Chris, Prue, John and
Pam for being as wonderful as ever.

Thank you to all of our clients for letting us help
them in their quest to become the best.

CONTENTS

INTRODUCTION

Hello and welcome to *How to Be the Best*.

We dogs have never understood why being the *best* is so hard for you humans, because to dogs it comes completely naturally.

But stop worrying, because your problems are over. Following in the footsteps of our highly esteemed pack leader Ludwig Von Dober-Weimaraner, who has already written the life-changing *Think Dog Rules for Life*, we have decided to sort you out and help you become the *best* you can possibly be.

Dogs know from a very early age that wanting to be the *best* is one thing, but being the *best* is quite another.

It doesn't matter whether a dog just wants to be their pets' (owners to you) *best* friend or whether they have far loftier ambitions such as becoming 'Best in Show' at Crufts.

However gorgeous or talented a dog is, success rarely falls into our laps. We know that if we want to be the *best* we must be relentlessly, exhaustingly determined and completely fixated on achieving our goals.

Take racing dogs, such as the huskies that pull sledges across the frozen snow of the north. These dogs combine tenacity, teamwork and endless practice to become the *best* in incredibly harsh conditions.

Then there are guide dogs, police dogs, army dogs and endless other specialists that train for years to achieve things that humans can only wonder at.

The difference between being the best and being second best lies in a dog's determination.

x

Over the years dogs have even won medals for bravery, saving countless humans from death and danger.

But the thread that runs through all these stories is one of aspiration, preparation, determination and perspiration combined with a detailed knowledge of and a healthy respect for their environment, the people and the animals that they are either competing against, trying to help or relying upon as they strive to be the *best* in their chosen field.

Everyone who reads this book and believes not only in what I am saying, but in themselves, has the power to be the *best*.

Look deep into yourself and discover what you can be *best* at, then the sky's the limit.

So the very *best* of luck to all of you and please, please let me know how you get on.

Be relentless, be faithful
and be the best!
Lots of love,
Oscar

xxxxxx

Email me at:
Oscar@thinkdog.net

Or visit:
www.thinkdog.net

Becoming Top Dog is a great start but a burning desire to stay Top Dog is what turns a good dog into a champion.

BEING THE BEST

A CHAMPION'S TALE

What does being the *best* actually mean?

Well, being the *best* isn't about quick fixes or scams to help you get rich quick.

Being the *best* means embarking on a long, hard, highly unpredictable road full of slip-ups, muddy slides and a few nasty falls.

Being the *best* isn't about achieving one single goal but about constantly, relentlessly setting out to achieve one hard-to-reach goal after another.

2

Being the *best* is about blood, sweat, tears and being prepared to put in long, lonely hours with absolutely no guarantee of any return. It is about knowing that every setback is actually a learning point for tomorrow and that the only real failure is giving up.

It's about having the confidence to describe the future as you see it, even when all the evidence is contradicting you, or others are too blind to see what you mean.

Being the *best* means taking risks, using every ounce of potential you were born with and still somehow finding something more to give. It means striving to do better even when, by other people's standards, you are doing well already.

To be the *best* you must start with an all-consuming desire to be the *best* and be prepared to exhaust yourself challenging and eventually overcoming all barriers to progress.

Be willing to win over or subdue your detractors, turn stumbling blocks into stepping stones and persevere way beyond the limits of other people.

Champions won't accept anything less than being the *best* and neither should you.

They are driven by an insatiable thirst for success and it's that thirst for success that gives them the will to persist – and it's their persistence that finally brings them their goal.

The harder a dog works,
the *better* it gets.

Look to a future beyond the horizons of other dogs.

BEST DIRECTION

BE EXTRAORDINARY NOT ORDINARY

If you want your dream to turn into your reality you must be able to describe it so clearly that anyone you share it with can close their eyes and feel the fur on its back, smell its wonderful aroma or taste its yummy flavour with the same passion and excitement that you can.

Does even thinking about your vision for the future make your mouth water? Can you make other people drool with excitement when you describe the future?

Because you need to!

OPPORTUNITY KNOCKS

Opportunity favours the prepared mind, so here are five key pointers to prepare you for life's great adventure.

PURPOSE

Describe the wonderful thing you want to achieve. What makes it special and unique?

Is it ambitious enough to be worthy of you and your friends? What won't happen if you don't make it happen?

PROMISE

Have you looked at things from other people's perspectives?

Why should anyone else be bothered? What are the benefits and what's the payback?

Why should people believe in **you** rather than someone else with a similar idea?

Expect to become the
stick against which all
other dogs are measured.

GOALS

If you want to make things happen you need goals.

How many bones or biscuits? Who's going to do what, who gets what and when do you expect to cut to the chase?

You must have clear priorities, success measures, targets, timescales and an effective way of reviewing progress before you start – or how will anyone be able to tell how far you've got, how close you are to reaching your goal or what still needs to be done to make sure that you get there?

BEHAVIOURS

If you want to create a winning team or encourage people to trust you as an individual (or maybe you just want to trust yourself more), then you must exhibit consistent behaviours and attitudes.

How do the winners in your chosen area behave? What separates the champions from the runners up?

Describe the behaviours you want your pack to exhibit. Do you demonstrate them yourself?

Are you sure?

It's vital that you do if you want others to follow you.

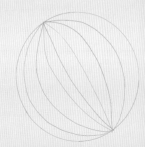

STYLE

Compared to dogs, humans are not the most imaginative of animals, so if you want people to 'totally get it' then turn your idea into a Technicolor movie not a textbook!

How do you want people to see you? What matters? Is it: size, colour, space, simplicity, emphasis, pictures or illustration?

Remember that pictures tell a thousand words so always think about your messages visually.

The way you use words can be amazingly powerful, so use them wisely. How do you want people to hear you?

What do you want your voice to sound like?

Once you have thought about all this, test it with people you trust and then test it with your target audience.

Study the ways of great
dogs.

BEST LEADERSHIP

THE LEADERSHIP CHALLENGE

Now that you have a direction, how about your leadership potential? Will you be able to lead **yourself** to the Promised Land, let alone persuade anyone else to follow you?

The road to Hell is paved with good intentions and the sad news is that more humans fall at the second hurdle of 'Best Leadership' than at the first one, 'Best Direction'.

So let me share the secrets of great leadership with you: focus, focus, focus; communication, communication, communication. Doesn't sound that hard does it?

Do everything you can to keep yourself and your team, if you have one, mentally and physically together.

KEEP ONE EYE OPEN AT ALL TIMES!

A great leader like Ludwig misses nothing and lets nothing go – he even sleeps with one eye open.

He doesn't tolerate even a single degree of variation from what the pack has agreed to, because he knows that if he does, what starts off as a one-degree variation will rapidly become a 180-degree disagreement.

Think about it like this:

* great leadership ensures discipline,
* discipline delivers focus,
* focus delivers trust,
* trust creates energy,
* energy spots opportunity,
* opportunity creates success,
* success delivers rewards.

But remember: too many rewards can lead you to lose your discipline and focus, and then you will stop being the *best*.

How great a dog do you
aspire to be?

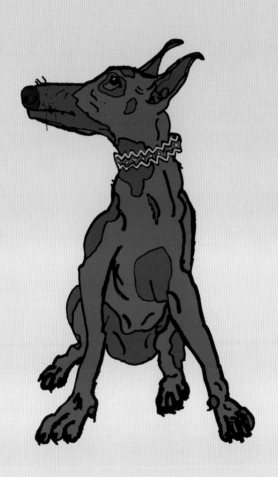

CREATING A FOLLOWING

There is only one way to stay true to yourself and create a lead worthy of being followed, and that is through truth, proof, evidence and demonstration.

Whatever you believe in, stick to it.

Demonstrate your core beliefs in every word you utter and every action you take.

As Ludwig says, *'A dog must always be a dog, even in a cattery'*.

If you can also manage to provide proof and evidence of everything that you need other people to believe in, then you will become a leader that even Ludwig would be proud to associate with.

And here's something else you need to know: winners and great leaders stick together like glue, so earn yourself membership of the *'winners pack'* and you won't look back.

A lone dog will never be as strong as a pack.

BEST RELATIONSHIPS

THE FORGOTTEN ART OF RELATIONSHIPS

In this age of disposable everything, one of the few things with enduring value will be your relationships. Dogs know this, because we rely solely on the strength of our relationships to survive. Without them we would be out on the streets.

But you humans seem to have lost the plot a bit when it comes to relationships, and forgotten some of the things that helped you get out of caves and swamps and into houses and cities.

Whether it is relationships between family members, colleagues or even organisations and countries, you may be in danger of paying less attention to relationships than they deserve and require.

MAKING TIME FOR PEOPLE

Relationships are what separate out talented runners-up from champions.

The world's most successful people and the world's most successful dogs know that the route to long-term success and being the *best* lies fairly and squarely through establishing and maintaining great, long-lasting, personal relationships.

This is how they get to hear about new opportunities before others.

This is how they learn to recognise opportunity when they see it.

This is also how they get the best out of the people upon whose help and support they rely to turn opportunities into realities.

IT'S NOT WHAT YOU KNOW; IT'S WHO YOU KNOW

It may not be fair but life isn't fair, so if you or your team want to be the *best* you had better make sure that you get to know the people that matter.

* Champions rely on their networks.

* Leaders rely on their networks.

* Socialites rely on their networks.

* Dogs live and die by their pack hierarchy and networks.

So what are you doing to build up your network and invest in the relationships you need to be the *best*?

Who do you still need to get to know?

Make a plan to get to know them.

A happy dog has a
thousand friends.

BEST COMMUNICATION

Whatever you are trying to be the *best* at, regardless of whether you are an individual, a team or a whole country, you will only ever become the *best* at it once you have become a master communicator.

As a rule of thumb, try this. Work out who you want to communicate with as part of becoming the *best* (usually more people than you first think), then decide how much effort you need to put into communicating with them.

Now multiply this estimate by 20 and you will be about right. It is incredible how much effort champions put into communicating, but they do it because they know that without it they'll only ever be just another mid-table player.

A dog will only become the top dog if it believes it's the top dog from the start.

Now you have an idea how much effort you need to put into communicating, how should you set about it?

PUT YOURSELF IN THE ZONE

Before you think about talking to anyone remember that passion, belief and total conviction are the only viable launch pad for any potential communicator.

Get yourself into a frenzy of uncontrollable excitement and you are ready for the off.

INSPIRE

Transmit your own excitement and personal belief before you start explaining the detail of your dream, and make sure that your audience is excited about you before they start considering your idea.

PAINT

Paint a picture of your vision: tell stories, use analogies, use parables, make it personal to you and, even more importantly, personal to them.

Sell the aroma, sell the sizzle, and only then let them see the sausage!

IMMERSE

Don't just communicate; immerse people into your dream until it flows around them, over them and ultimately through them.

EVANGELISE

Word of mouth is a thousand times more powerful than anything else, so get out there and be relentless. Tell them what you want to tell them, tell them, tell them what you've told them and then tell them again.

KISS YOUR WAY TO GREATNESS

Apart from being great fun, kissing (or as we dogs prefer, licking) your way to greatness is the only way to do it.

KISS – keep it simple, stupid.

Project a strong, memorable personality – nobody likes grey people.

Greet and involve EVERYONE and speak to everyone personally.

Fixate on a few easy-to-remember themes.

Take EVERY chance you get to get your messages across.

And repeat yourself until (like me) you are blue in the face!

It's hard
to forget
a truly great
dog.

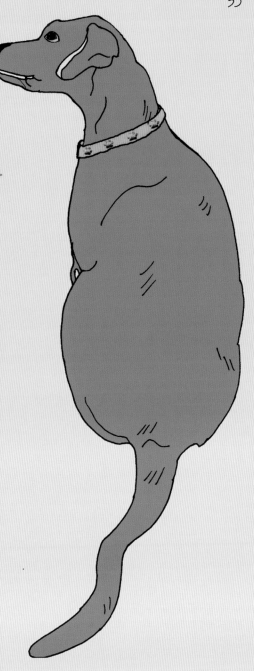

GET IT STRAIGHT

This is the profile of champions – people who are the *best* at what they do.

* Highly visible – champions make sure they get everywhere so start putting yourself about.

* Respected – champions are respected by their peers.

* Authoritative – champions are commanding.

* Clear – champions are clear and concise.

* Opinionated – you can't be half a champion and it's the same when it comes to having a view about something within your key area of expertise; tell it as it is. (But remember that this only applies to the things you're *best* at and certainly not to everything else!)

Any dog can have its day if it enters the right competition!

BEST TALENT

Talent is the holy grail of being the *best* because without talent you won't even make it out of the kennel.

But can you spot talent in others?

Indeed, can you spot your *own* talents?

We are all incredibly talented, but problems will arise if we don't know where our talent lies, if we stop believing that we are talented or if we are simply hell-bent on a dream to which our own talents are not best suited.

Everyone on this planet is a potential champion at something, so find out what you are *best* at and start believing in yourself.

BECOME A TALENT GROUPIE

Talent is without doubt one of the most exciting, rejuvenating and uplifting ingredients of life, but spotting talent is a mindset that you must actively get yourself into.

Start by celebrating talent in yourself and others.

CREATE A TALENT WHIRLWIND

Talent itself is a talent magnet because raw talent attracts other raw talent. Seek out people who are using their talents to great effect, learn from them, be inspired by them and share your dreams together.

HONE YOUR TALENT

Great teams need coaches; football teams don't fire their coach when they win the Champions League, for example. They know they need to keep learning even when they've reached the top.

Take every opportunity to learn from others, whilst also helping them express and develop **their** talent.

BECOME A TALENT INCUBATOR

Like plum blossom in an Evesham orchard, talent is delicate. Latent talent can grow into a fruitful, resilient tree but, like blossom, a late frost can kill it in its tracks.

If you want your talent to reach maturity, you must nurture and protect it.

Champion dogs never
stop learning new tricks.

Genuinely talented
dogs learn to sniff out
the tastiest morsels.

LIBERATE TALENT

What song does your talent dance to?

Can you make people dance to your tune?

What do you need to do to liberate every succulent ounce of talent that exists deep inside the marrow of your bones and those of everyone around you?

Remember: bury bones but liberate talent.

If a dog isn't in trouble from time to time, it isn't playing hard enough!

MY FRIENDS AND I

How to Be the Best showcases the combined wisdom of the 24 wonderful, mischievous, fun-loving dogs and two insightful cats that make up our pack.

As well as being able to call upon such a wide range of skills and experiences, I have been lucky enough to have the support and advice of our leader, Ludwig Von Dober-Weimaraner, a true great of the canine world whom I am privileged to be able to call a friend as well as our esteemed pack leader.

So a big thanks to all my canine chums, (especially Lucy for her late-night encouragement), for their invaluable input and help without which this book would not have been possible.

You really are the *best* of friends!

ABOUT WILL AND ANNALESE

Cofounders of business troubleshooters and relationship specialists Murray Murray (www.murraymurray.com) and Family Firms, (www.familyfirms.net), Will and Annalese Murray have been helping people and organisations to be the *best* for many years now.

Previous clients include:

- Orange, Fujitsu, British Energy, Glaxo Smith Kline, RWE nPower and several Government agencies;

- various trusts, charities, educational institutions and schools as well as family businesses and private individuals.

Previous books include: *Think Dog: Rules for Life* (Friendly Publishing); *Corporate Denial* (Capstone); *Hey You* (Momentum); and *Brand Storm* (Financial Times, Prentice Hall).

THINK DOG

RULES FOR LIFE

Will and Annalese Murray

Why do humans take a simple thing like being everyone's best friend and make it so hard?

This has been troubling dogs for years. In fact, seeing humans suffer has become so upsetting that Ludwig has decided to take the plunge and share his amazing doggy secrets with you, the human race.

Proven over thousands of years of doggie desirability, Ludwig's *Think Dog Rules for Life* will help you to:

* get more out of life and love;
* be more popular and self confident;
* respond positively to all types of bullying;
* make a bigger difference in the world;
* be happier;
* improve every area of your life;
* change your life forever.

Already widely renowned as the world's best canine life and relationship coach, Ludwig is now ready, willing and able to help you.

For more information on Think Dog visit
www.thinkdog.net